Towards a Social History of Early Modern Dutch

Towards a Social History of Early Modern Dutch

Peter Burke

AMSTERDAM UNIVERSITY PRESS

The Meertens Ethnology Cahiers are revised texts of the Meertens Ethnology Lectures. These lectures are presented by ground-breaking researchers in the field of ethnology and related disciplines at the Meertens Institute in Amsterdam, a research facility in language and culture in the Netherlands

The Meertens Institute is a research institute of the Royal Netherlands Academy of Arts and Sciences

Meertens Institute
Department of Ethnology
PO Box 94264
1090 GG Amsterdam
www.meertens.knaw.nl

Meertens Ethnology Cahier 1
Series Editor: Peter Jan Margry
peter.jan.margry@meertens.knaw.nl

Illustration front cover: Adriaen van Ostade, *Rustende reizigers*, 36 x 30 cm.
© Rijksmuseum, Amsterdam
Illustration back cover: Peter Burke during Meertens Ethnology Lecture (photo by Theo Meder)

Cover design: Kok Korpershoek, Amsterdam
Lay out: JAPES, Amsterdam

ISBN 90 5356 861 1

© Amsterdam University Press, 2005

All rights reserved. Without limiting the rights under copyright reserved above, no part of this book may be reproduced, stored in or introduced into a retrieval system, or transmitted, in any form or by any means (electronic, mechanical, photocopying, recording or otherwise) without the written permission of both the copyright owner and the author of the book.

Why is a foreigner writing about Dutch and a historian writing about language? The point is that I am a firm believer in the value of the social history of language.[1] I am also convinced that there is much work of this kind still to be done in the case of Dutch. Hence the word 'towards' in the title, emphasizing that what follows is a survey of territory that has not been fully mapped, and that its conclusions are necessarily provisional.*

'Dutch' may not actually be the best term for the language variously described at the time and since as *Belgisch*, *Nederlands*, *Nederduits*, *Neerduits*, or '*goed platen duytsche*', not to mention regional variations such as *Vlaams*, *Brabants*, *Hollands*, *Limburgs*, and so on.[2] It might be a good idea to speak of 'dutches' in the plural, as some linguists now speak of englishes.[3] All the same, here I shall follow normal usage and continue to use the term in the singular, without forgetting to discuss changes in the southern or Spanish Netherlands as well as in the North.[4] Before turning to Dutch, though, it may be useful to define the approach described here as the social history of language.

The social history of language is also known as the historical sociology (or anthropology) of language, or as socio-historical linguistics. As these different names suggest, the 'field' is actually more like a crossroads between disciplines, with all the opportunities that the metaphor of the crossroads implies both for encounters as well as for misunderstanding directions and losing one's way. The essential point of this enterprise is to combine social with historical studies of language, focusing on the relation between language and society, or more precisely, between languages and communities. So far as evidence permits – a major difficulty, to be discussed in a moment – the social approach privileges spoken over written language, simply because there was and is so much more of it and because it involves everyone rather than a literate minority.[5]

But what counts as a social approach? The term is an ambiguous one. For some historians, the phrase 'social history' has a relatively precise and narrow meaning: the history of changes in the social structure. For other scholars, the phrase has a wide meaning that is virtually synonymous with 'cultural history'. Writers on the history of English, for instance, use the two terms more or less interchangeably.[6]

My own preference is for the term 'social', on the grounds that language is necessarily a cultural phenomenon. To speak of a cultural history of dreams, for example, or gesture, or humour, is a useful reminder that dreams, gestures and jokes are cultural as well as natural phenomena and that they vary from place to place and from one period to another. In the case of language, on the other hand, given the diversity of tongues, the reminder is surely unnecessary. To define the social history of language, I shall follow Joshua Fishman or Leopold Peeters, who translated Fishman's well-known formula, 'who speaks what language to whom and when', as 'wie spreekt welke taal tot wie, wanneer, over welk onderwerp en met welke bedoeling' ('who speaks what language to whom and when; what is the subject matter being spoken of, and with what intention is it being spoken').[7]

Any attempt to analyse the relation between language and society raises some very large general questions or debates, including the relative importance of internal and external approaches and of rival explanations in terms of structure or agency.[8]

Like historians of art, science, music and other disciplines, scholars working on the history of language may be divided into internalists and externalists, though some try to combine the two approaches. On one side, there are the scholars who place the emphasis on language as a system of interdependent parts that develops or 'evolves', as linguists like Otto Jespersen used to say, according to its own logic in a sequence of necessary stages. On the other side, we find linguists, sociologists and historians who concern themselves mainly with the relation between language and the rest of the culture or society – with religion, with politics, with social class, with gender and so on.

In what follows, external factors will dominate the discussion, since a social history of language is external by definition. To say this does not mean denying the importance of internal factors: the point is one about the division of intellectual labour. I view the internal and external approaches as complementary, not contradictory. In any case, the social approach should not be pursued in a narrow or exclusive spirit. In order to know where to draw a line, it is necessary to go beyond it.

There remains the difficult problem of deciding what factors to count as internal or external. In one sense – the geographical – the influence of French on Dutch is external; in another sense – the disciplinary sense – the influence of French is internal to language, as opposed to external factors such as war or immigration. The point is essentially a relative one.

It is particularly important not to identify the external history of language with the history of words, and the internal history with grammar and syntax. Words may be borrowed from outside for internal reasons, because the language lacks or needs them. Conversely, it should be possible to present a sociology or social history of grammar whenever different grammatical forms happen to be associated with different social groups. Whether or not this is the case in a given place or time is obviously a matter for empirical investigation, not for a decision taken in advance.

Another major debate in the history of language, as in other kinds of history (not to mention sociology and anthropology), is the one between the 'structuralists' and the supporters of human agency. It may look like a continuation of the first debate, but the two discussions are not symmetrical. In this second debate we find one group of scholars offering explanations of linguistic change in terms of an 'invisible hand', including not only the internal evolution of the language but also external, impersonal trends such as the rise of the nation-state. On the other side, we find linguists who emphasize the speakers rather than the language, stressing the strategies and the actions of individuals and groups.[9]

In this debate it is surely necessary to strive for a reconciliation or synthesis between the two approaches. The case of neologisms shows how this synthesis might work. If neologisms are the work of individuals, some of whose names we know, the fate of these neologisms lies outside their control. It is the group or community that decides whether a given innovation will be successful – voting with their mouths, by adopting or resisting it. Hence some of the neologisms coined by Stevin, for example, were adopted, while others fell by the wayside.

Simon Stevin (1548-1620).
Photo: Iconografisch Bureau / RKD, The Hague

II

Adding history to society and language raises yet another acute problem, at least in the case of the age before the invention of the tape recorder: the problem of sources for the spoken language. It may be useful to distinguish five of these sources: treatises on language, plays, informal letters, charters and records of interrogations.

Lambert ten Kate (1674-1731) by Jacob Houbraken.
Photo: Iconografisch Bureau / RKD, The Hague

Treatises on language are an obvious source. However, like conduct books in the case of the history of everyday life, these treatises need to be read against the grain in the sense of treating discussions of how not to speak as a means of discovering the way in which people actually spoke. The use that has been made of Lambert ten Kate, a 'sociolinguist avant la lettre' in order to reconstruct eighteenth-century Dutch sociolects offers a striking example of this strategy, even if it may be criticized as impressionistic, its conclusions sometimes at variance with studies of a large corpus of evidence.[10] A similar point might be made about the testimony of dictionaries, notably the famous dictionary compiled by Cornelius Kiliaan, *Etymologicum teutonicae linguae* (1574).

There is also a danger of anachronism in describing Ten Kate in this way, and the differences between his observations and the more systematic approach followed by sociolinguists in the last half-century need to be made clear. But it would be even more misleading to imagine that the sociolinguistics of the 1950s was based on completely new insights.

Plays are at once a richer and a more problematic source. If Shakespeare, Lope de Vega, Molière, Goldoni and Holberg had not written, the social histories of English, Spanish, French, Venetian and Danish would be much impoverished. In the case of Dutch, scholars have turned to the comedies of Constantijn Huygens, Samuel Coster and, above all, of Gerbrand Bredero ('onze rijkste bron', according to Daan) for information about varieties of language in the seventeenth century.[11]

Can the testimony of playwrights be trusted? We obviously have to avoid reading the texts too literally. Allowances have to be made for exaggeration, for stylization and for satire. All the same, the satire would not be effective if the audience did not recognize the dialect, in other words, if some people had not been speaking in more or less the manner of, for example, Molière's *Précieuses ridicules* or Bredero's *Hispanicized Brabanter*.

In contrast to treatises and plays, other sources for the history of early modern spoken Dutch have not been studied as exhaustively as they might be. Private letters for example, 'familiar' letters as they were called at the time, especially the letters of relatively humble people, are likely to have kept close to the manner in which the writers spoke. Many letters from Dutch sailors to their families or vice versa have survived and they might be used to reconstruct the history of ordinary language and of other aspects of the everyday life of the period.[12]

Again, in the case of the writer P.C. Hooft, it has been pointed out more than once than in his letters he switched codes according to the intended recipient, moving between a more formal style containing more Latin and French words and a plainer and more colloquial Dutch.[13] Polite forms of address have recently been studied by linguists via seventeenth-century letters.[14]

Charters are another valuable source for the history of the spoken language, at least for the Middle Ages. As in the case of Old French, so in that of Middle Dutch a systematic comparison between the spellings of words in charters and in literary texts reveals that some of these literary texts are representations of dialects (assuming that spelling conventions are at least a rough equivalent of a phonetic record).[15]

Trials, too, offer a rich source for the history of the spoken language. In the Catholic world – in Italy, Spain and Portugal, for instance – one thinks of interrogations by inquisitors of ordinary people under suspicion of heresy and of the instructions to the clerks to write down everything the suspect said, including cries of pain under torture. Despite the absence of an inquisition, the interrogations of witnesses in court might be used as a source for the history of language in the Netherlands too. In this area, social historians, already familiar with this kind of document, might draw the attention of linguists to particularly rich or unusual texts.

III

A number of important studies have been published on the relation between the Dutch language and the societies and cultures in which it has been spoken and written. A few of these studies go back a century or more.[16] Indeed, a valuable overview was published as long ago as the 1930s: C.G.N. de Vooys's *Geschiedenis van de Nederlandse taal*.[17]

De Vooys's book is a successful attempt to place the history of language within more general history (religious and political in this case, rather than social in the strict sense). Naturally enough, after three-quarters of a century, the book looks dated in some respects. For example, the author says little about women. Vooys also has little to say about the phenomenon of diglossia (a term he does not use), or about the interaction between the different languages used in the Netherlands – Frisian, French, Latin, German and so on.[18]

More recently, a number of linguists in the Netherlands have concerned themselves with both society and history, among them Jo Daan and Leopold Peeters, while a few historians, notably Willem Frijhoff, have also turned in this direction.[19]

More recent surveys, all of them more concerned with social change than Vooys, include: a history of Dutch by Marijke van der Wal and Cor Bree, which combines internal and external approaches; a history of Dutch in the Southern Netherlands by Roland Willemyns, which concentrates on external factors; and two studies of the standardization of language, one an essay on the period around 1650 by Van der Wal, the other a richly detailed study of the rise of standard Dutch (*Algemeen Beschaafd Nederlands* or ABN) by Nicoline van der Sijs.[20]

My hope is that this brief account of themes in the social history of Dutch may help to encourage further studies in this country, whether by individuals or by teams (there is already a group working on the social history of Flemish at the Free University in Brussels).[21] To take advantage of being an outsider, I shall present what I consider to be the principal problems from a comparative perspective, concentrating on five problems in particular: i) the so-called 'rise of the vernacular'; ii) the standardization of language; iii) language mixing; iv) language purification; and v) sectorial languages.

What follows, then, is a review of the literature, surveying and appraising the work that has been done so far in each of these five areas.

I shall make comparisons and contrasts between studies of early modern Dutch and studies of other languages, attempting to identify future directions of research, areas in which research is particularly needed, and areas in which social historians can make a particularly useful contribution to a common or co-operative enterprise.

IV

It has often been argued that the early modern period – continuing a trend that goes back in the case of Dutch to the thirteenth century – was one of the 'emergence', the 'rise' or the 'triumph' of the national vernaculars at the expense of cosmopolitan Latin on the one hand and local dialects on the other.

The praises of the Dutch language were often sung in the course of the Renaissance, with Stevin's *Uytspraeck vande weerdigheyt der Duytsche tael* (1586) and the *Twe-Spraack vande Nederduitsche Letterkunst* (1584) by Hendrik Spieghel and his *rederijker* colleagues as the most famous examples of a more general trend that included contributions by Jan Gymnick, Erycius Puteanus, Petrus Scriverius and others.[22] The genre was a European one in the early modern period, in which Dutch humanists followed their Italian, Spanish, Portuguese and French colleagues and preceded the English, the Germans, the Swedes and so on.

Where Stevin wrote of the 'wealth' (*rijcheyt*) of Dutch, Joachim Du Bellay, Richard Mulcaster and Marcin Siennik and other writers made the same point about French, English, Polish and other languages.[23] Indeed, the *Twe-Spraack* cited the examples of the Italians, the French and the English to support the argument that Netherlanders should take pride in their language.

What we see in the Netherlands – as indeed elsewhere in Europe – is not only multilingualism, the co-existence between languages, but also competition for territory: or to make the same point in the language of agency, a number of speakers attempting to impose their own language in particular domains.[24] The gradual expansion of

Dutch at the expense of French in the political domain is well known, with 1477 (when Dutch replaced French as the official language of the county of Holland and Zeeland following the death of Charles the Bold) and 1582 (when Dutch became the language of the States-General) as important milestones in this development.[25]

The gradual expansion of Dutch at the expense of Latin in the domain of writing and print is another familiar story. Dutch also expanded at the expense of Frisian, to become the language of church, towns and elites, although there was resistance to the trend: the poet Gysbert Japicx published his *Fryske Rymerije* as late as 1668.[26]

Dutch was also expanding elsewhere in Europe, into the Baltic and even into Britain.[27] Although the English have almost forgotten this now, Dutch could be heard in the streets of Norwich and probably other East Anglian towns in the seventeenth and eighteenth centuries, thanks to the immigration in the later sixteenth century of Protestants fleeing persecution. The interaction between the two languages even led to changes in the grammar of spoken English in the region, notably the distinctive third person singular.[28] Again, when the Scottish clergyman Gilbert Burnet met Peter the Great, the language in which they conversed was Dutch.

Dutch was probably the Western language that a Russian of this time was most likely to know. In the seventeenth and eighteenth centuries, the new Russian naval vocabulary was mainly Dutch, including *anker, konvooi, matroos, mast, stuurboord* and *zeil*. Russian terms referring to trade and finance were also derived from Dutch, among them *actie, bankroet, beurs, dividend, kantoor* and *kwitantie*.[29] Like the use of Italian business terms in German, English, French and other languages in the sixteenth century, the spread of Dutch economic terminology reflected their economic hegemony.[30]

Looking into the future from the early seventeenth century, Dutch might well have appeared to have better prospects than English. The rise of the Dutch seaborne empire was spreading the language to East and Southeast Asia, South Africa, North America and for a generation, to the northeast of Brazil as well.[31]

For example, over three hundred Dutch words entered Japanese in the Edo period, of which about half are still in use, including naval terms such as 'madorosu' (*matroos*) and 'masuto' (*mast*), as well as 'biiru' (*bier*), 'garasu' (*glas*) and 'kohii' (*koffie*). In eighteenth-century Japan, Dutch learning ('Rangaku', from 'Oranda', Holland) was synonymous with Western learning and the first Western scientific book translated into Japanese was a Dutch treatise on anatomy.[32] It must have been quite a shock for the Japanese when they realized that Dutch was not the principal European language.

All the same, Dutch failed to root itself in most of these places in the manner of its rival, Portuguese, despite occasional efforts by representatives of the VOC. In 1641, for instance, an edict of the Governor-General of the East Indies ruled that slaves were only allowed to wear hats or caps if they knew Dutch, the idea being, apparently, to create a linguistic bond between colonizers and colonized. The scheme seems to have failed. Again, in 1659, the Governor of Colombo ordered slaves to learn Dutch, once more to little avail. The one success story was the rise of Afrikaans, presumably because the Dutch went to South Africa as settlers rather than as traders or administrators. Even in this case, the language is more or less restricted to descendants of the original settlers, its use as a lingua franca discouraged by its associations with a former oppressive regime.[33]

In the struggle for territory there were losses as well as gains, as the examples of French and Latin show. French increased its hold in the seventeenth century as the spoken and written language of the upper classes in the Dutch Republic (curiously enough, what has been called 'la francisation de l'élite flamande' occurred a century later, as it would, of course, in the German-speaking world and in Russia).[34] What remain to be investigated are the occasions on which French was used – speaking to whom, where and about what, to return to Fishman's formula.

Despite the praises of the vernacular, Latin remained the language of most of the Netherlanders who participated in the Republic of Letters as it was of a substantial minority of books published in the Dutch Republic in the early modern period (there are about 33,000 items in Latin listed in the Royal Library's *Short Title Catalogue*, compared to about 12,000 in French and about 84,000 in Dutch. Of the 550 translators from vernacular languages into Latin in the early modern period who are known to me, 48 came from the Netherlands.[35]

In practice, although the famous physician Isaac Beeckmann favoured Dutch as the language of instruction in physics for craftsmen, and Stevin lectured in that language, there was little space for the vernacular in Dutch universities. The suggestion made by a chamber of rhetoric ('In Liefde Bloeiende') in 1585 that the vernacular should be used for teaching at Leiden University seems to have met with no response.[36]

V

One of the major trends in the history of early modern Dutch, as of early modern Italian, French, Spanish and English (and to a lesser extent other languages as well) was standardization, a term here used in the sense of members of a group (nation, class) coming to speak in a similar manner.[37] The process was of course incomplete in the period – it is not complete even today – but the trend is obvious enough.

The process of standardization was encouraged by two major socio-cultural trends of the time, urbanization and the rise of printing. Antwerp and Amsterdam in particular, like other large cities, Paris and London for instance, were melting-pots of dialects as they were of local customs in general.[38] The importance in the history of language of the emigration from South to North after 1585 has often been pointed out. Irritating to traditional Amsterdammers as it may have been at the time (as Bredero's famous satire on the Spanish Brabanter suggests), the language of the immigrants made an important contribution to the formation of what became standard Dutch.[39] By contrast the dialects of the eastern Netherlands made relatively little contribution to the standard, though more than used to be thought.[40] Why? These dialects lacked prestige.[41] A social historian might explain this lack of prestige by the lack of important towns in the region, and *a fortiori*, by the lack of writers and printers there.

The multiplication and spread of printed texts in the vernacular also encouraged standardization. In her well-known work on the contribution of the press to social and cultural change in early modern Europe, Elizabeth Eisenstein stressed the importance of the standardization of texts. Recent scholars have argued that Eisenstein exaggerated this trend and noted what they call the 'instability' of printed texts that were corrected sheet by sheet during the printing process so that no two copies of the 'same' text are identical.[42] However, this point qualifies or weakens Eisenstein's argument rather than rebutting it altogether.

In the case of language, the argument that printing promoted standardization is particularly strong. In the case of Spanish, English and German, scholars have compared the manuscript with the printed versions of certain books to show how printers eliminated idiosyncratic or regional spellings.[43] We might speak of the 'logic' of print in the sense that in order to make a profit, printers needed to standardize texts to make them intelligible to as large a number of readers as possible.[44]

In the case of Dutch, when the poems of the fifteenth-century Bruges rhetorician Anthonis de Roovere came to be printed in the sixteenth century, a number of spellings were changed; *cuenynck* became *coninck*, *up* became *op*, *souckt* became *soeckt* and so on, approximating modern usage in most cases.[45] In fact, Philips van Marnix of Sint Aldegonde had already noted the influence of print on the written language when in the preface to his translation of the Psalms he noted how the printers encouraged the replacement of *du* by *ghy*.[46]

Standardization should not be viewed as an automatic or a purely impersonal process. In the case of urbanization, the term refers to the unintended collective consequences of intentional individual actions such as the decision to immigrate. In the case of print, we should be thinking and speaking of the role of individual printers as well as that of the 'press' as agents of change. For example, Roovere's poems were edited by the sixteenth-century Antwerp printer Jan van Ghelen, or someone working for him. It was they who decided on the changes that have just been cited as examples of a general trend. In other words, conscious attempts at standardization must not be forgotten, even if they required an alliance with impersonal forces such as urbanization and print in order to achieve some degree of success.

One important reason for conscious standardization was economic, but another was religious. In the Netherlands as in other parts of Europe, the diversity of dialects was perceived as an obstacle to the spread of the Gospel. Luther translated the Bible not into his own Saxon dialect but (following the example of the Saxon chancery) into a kind of *koine* that drew on different dialects. The early modern translators of the Bible into Swedish and Finnish had a similar aim, to be achieved by regional representation on the team of translators.[47]

In the case of Dutch, a number of attempts were made to translate the Bible into a *koine* or *gemeyn spraeck*. The preface to a translation of the New Testament published in 1525 declared that the translator's aim was to find a middle way between *Hollants* and *Brabants*.[48] Again, Jan Utenhove's *New Testament* aimed at 'a Dutch text which would be comprehensible to readers from all parts of the Netherlands'.[49] The *Statenbijbel* (1637) was the work of a committee in which, as in Sweden and Finland, different regions were represented. Its influence on the Dutch language, spoken as well as written, has often been noted, though some recent accounts are more sceptical than their predecessors.[50]

Despite these efforts, a common language was long in coming. In the eighteenth century, Adriaan Verwer was still calling for what he called a *lingua communis* or 'Gemeene-Lants-Tale'.[51] Although a number of plans to reform Dutch orthography had been proposed in the sixteenth and seventeenth centuries (often following the practice of the speaker's own region), for effective change it was necessary to wait until 1804, when Siegenbeek's suggestions had the support of the *Bataafsche Maatschappij van Taal- en Dichtkunde* and were followed by the introduction of uniform spelling by the *Staatsbewind der Bataafsche Republiek* on 18 December.[52]

Title page of the first edition of the *Statenbijbel*, printed in Leiden in 1637.
Photo: Dutch Bible Society Haarlem

On this delay, two comments may be in order. In the first place, the use of French by the upper classes probably delayed the rise of a standardized vernacular in the Netherlands as it did in Germany, since it made a high form of the spoken vernacular less necessary than elsewhere for distinguishing between people of high and low status.

In the second place, in the case of Dutch there was no equivalent of London or Paris as a linguistic model which combined the prestige of the court with that of a large city. In the seventeenth century, the form of language spoken 'in 's Gravenhage, de Raetkamer der Heeren Staten, en het hof van hunnen Stedehouder' was thought by some people, including Vondel, to be a model, together with Amsterdam, 'de maghtighste koopstadt der weerelt'.[53] However, these are two models, not one.

In any case, this model only extended to the United Provinces. If we look at the old 17 provinces of the Low Countries as a whole, there is evidence of increasing cultural divergence between North and South in the seventeenth century – more exactly, from the 1580s onwards – notably in religion and in art. It is plausible to suggest that this divergence, a contrast to the situation in both France and England, extended to language as well. In the South, there does not seem to have been any standard, so the choice was between speaking French or Spanish and speaking dialect. As F. Costerius complained in 1616, 'de moeders spraecke in 't selve land seer verscheyden is; een iegelyck bemindt ende prijst syns moeders taele ende misprijst d'andere'.[54] Divergence was made still sharper by the fact that the language of the United Provinces was open to influences from the seaborne empire, while that of the Spanish Netherlands was not.[55]

VI

The competition and interaction between vernaculars described earlier led to increased language mixing, just as the competition and interaction between dialects encouraged the emergence of a *koine*.[56] Language mixing in the Netherlands in particular was encouraged by the prevalence of multilingual individuals, since the different languages spoken by such individuals generally 'interfere' with (in other words, influence) one another.

Foreign visitors such as Ludovico Guicciardini regularly commented on the linguistic skills of Netherlanders. The English traveller Fynes Moryson, himself no mean performer in this respect, commented on 'the Flemings general skill in strange languages'. It is not difficult to cite instances of this skill. The ambassador Ogier Ghiselin de Busbecq spoke six modern languages – Dutch, German, Italian, Spanish, French and Croat – besides writing a famous account of the Ottoman Empire in Latin. Rubens corresponded in four languages: Italian, French, Spanish and Flemish. The Ghent patrician Karel Utenhove published a book of poems in twelve languages. In the Dutch Republic, Constantijn Huygens and his sons are said to have 'read Latin, French, Italian, Spanish, English, German and Dutch'.[57]

The rise of the printing press and the rise of migration both facilitated encounters between languages and the consequent 'contamination'. The two trends came together in sixteenth-century Antwerp, where printers produced books in French, German, Spanish and English as well as Latin and Flemish. As for seventeenth-century Amsterdam, its printers had a linguistic repertoire between them that included not only French, English, Spanish and German, but also Yiddish, Polish, Russian, Hungarian and Georgian. It was, for example, at Amsterdam that the Hungarian translation of a work of piety by the Cambridge Puritan William Perkins was printed in the early seventeenth century, like the Hungarian Bible in the late seventeenth century (printed by the Magyar immigrant Miklós Kis). We know that in multicultural cities today, certain words that once belonged to a particular ethnic group become more or less common property. It is likely that this was the case in early modern Amsterdam as well.

The expansion of the Dutch seaborne empire provided even more opportunities for languages to mix, including in this case the formation of pidgins and creoles.[58]

How many words were borrowed and from what languages? In this domain a statistical approach is sorely needed.[59] Even so, some

Dutch borrowings are clear enough, including some from non-European languages such as Arabic and Malay, borrowings studied by a number of scholars.[60] In the case of Europe, Dutch borrowed from Italian (in the domains of trade, art and music), from Spanish (in the domain of warfare) and, more generally, from French. The consequent sense of a cultural invasion, in the Netherlands as elsewhere in Europe, led to an increasing concern with purification.

VII

It is surely useful to distinguish linguistic standardization, the process by which members of a group come to speak in a similar manner, from purification, the conscious attempt to improve or ennoble the speech of individuals and groups (*verheerlijken* was a term used at the time). In this domain the emphasis necessarily falls on agents, even if the success or lack of success of their efforts depends in part on linguistic structures.

The language purification movements of the nineteenth and twentieth centuries, fuelled by nationalism, are well known.[61] In a recent book I argued for the importance of similar movements in the early modern period, from Spain to Iceland, although it is too early in these cases to speak of 'nationalism'. In the case of Dutch, there is a good deal to say about this topic.[62]

How then can the rise of a concern with linguistic purity be explained? To do so I drew on the work of the anthropologist Mary Douglas, who treats a stress on purity as a response to perceived danger, especially the danger to the cultural order posed by someone or something crossing its boundaries.[63] Although Douglas had little to say about language, her ideas help to explain the violence of some contemporary reactions to what was perceived as the invasion of the culture by words that came from the other side of a frontier.

Were the Dutch especially anxious about purity? Erasmus wrote a treatise on the purity of the Church. Menno Simons dreamed of a pure community 'without spot or stain'. In the seventeenth century, as Simon Schama has reminded us, foreign travellers regularly commented on the Dutch concern for clean streets and houses.[64] As for language, the concern with purity – among some writers and scholars at least – is clear enough, as the following examples will show, but it was not exceptional. In the seventeenth century in particular, Germans such as Johann Rist, Christian Gueintz and Justus Georg Schottel expressed similar anxieties about the invasion of their language by foreign and especially by French words.[65]

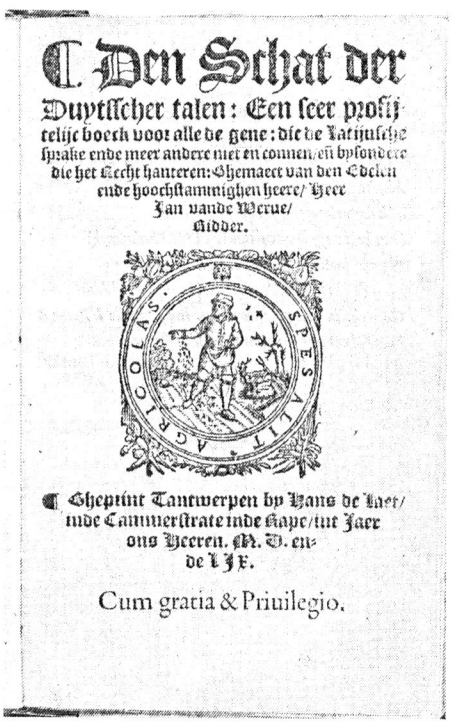

Den Schat der Duytsscher Talen (1559); the revised title of the second edition of *Tresoor der Duitsche Tale* (1553). Collection University Library Amsterdam

The Antwerp jurist Jan van de Werve, for instance, condemned the corruption of Dutch by Romance words in his *Tresoor der Duitsche Tale* (1553).[66] At that point he seems not to have noticed that the word *tresoor* was itself derived from the French *trésor*, an omission he put right in the second edition of his book, when the title was changed to the Germanic *Schat*. Spieghel, to return to him, argued against the use of French expressions such as *bon jour* in Dutch and against words of Latin origin such as *conscientie, disputatie* or *inventie*.

The purists used some vivid metaphors to make their point, beginning with 'purity' itself (*zuiverheid*). Again, from Spieghel in the sixteenth century to Antonides van der Goes and Joannes Vollenhove in the seventeenth, the influence of French, Latin and other languages on Dutch was described as producing *bastaardduits, basterdt-woorden, bastertspraak* or *bastertklank*.[67]

Another recurrent metaphor is the description of impure language as the 'scum' on the pot, by Matthijs de Castelein, for instance, in his book on rhetoric (1555), by Spieghel, who used the expression *schuymtalen* about Italian, Spanish, French and English.[68] Using another common metaphor, Justus van Effen criticized the mix of French and Dutch in his day as 'een sort van ragoutje'.[69]

What was to be done? Spieghel suggested that if borrowing had to take place at all, it should be from Germanic languages such as Frisian, Danish or even English. All the same, he preferred compounds of native words such as *twee-spraak* for 'dialogue'. In his coinages of mathematical and other technical terms, Stevin also preferred native compounds to borrowing from abroad; his word for 'triangle', for instance, was *driehoek* and for 'logic', *bewysconst*.[70]

Following the model of Stevin and others, the translator Jan Glazemaker devised native or native-sounding equivalents for the new philosophical terms, not only in his well-known version of Descartes but also in his translation of Guido Bentivoglio's history of the Dutch Revolt, in which a province is rendered *Lantschap*, a governor *Lantvoochd*, a secretary *Geheimschrijver*, a general *Opperhoofd*, a viceroy as *Onderkoning*, and so on.[71]

However, defensive purity is not the only form of purity. A Czech linguist, Jelínek, has distinguished between purism for defence and purism for prestige.[72] Norbert Elias's celebrated idea of a 'civilizing process' in early modern Europe might be extended to include attempts to reform language. Elias himself discussed the influence of the court of Versailles on French.[73] His follower, Joop Goudsblom, has written about the sociology of *Algemeen Beschaafd Nederlands* (a form of language perceived by its users as refined, urbane or 'polite') as a status symbol, a means to what Pierre Bourdieu called 'distinction'.[74]

In my view, there is another aspect to the question. Elias defined civilization in terms of self-control. One form of self-control, prevalent in religious circles in early modern Europe, was the conscious avoidance of swearing and indecent language, what the English Puritan William Perkins called 'the government of the tongue' (translated by Vincent Meusevoet in 1600 as *Eene onderwijsinghe voordraghende hoe men de tonge behoort te regeeren*). The concern was not a purely Protestant one: the Jesuit Carlo Rosignoli's treatise, *La lingua purgata* (1694) had a similar aim.

Another form of self-control, associated with the upper classes, stemmed from the concern with correct forms of address, a topic frequently discussed in conduct books.[75] Again, conversation, the subject of many early modern treatises, was, like riding and dancing, both an art and a form of bodily discipline, requiring its practitioners to learn not only how to speak but also when to remain silent. The importance of this linguistic aspect of good manners in early modern Europe has been stressed recently by scholars who use phrases such as 'the culture of conversation' or 'the civility of speech and writing'.[76]

Elias emphasized courts as linguistic models. Even in the Dutch Republic the court exercised some attraction, as Vondel pointed out. What linguists call the urbanization of language is even more obvious in the early modern period. The problem in the case of the Netherlands, in contrast to England and France, was which city to take as a linguistic model. Following his praise of The Hague, Vondel also recommended the speech of Amsterdam for imitation.

What about the South? According to Costerius, as we have seen, there was no model there. But if we follow Elias, we would expect the language of the court in Brussels (not Dutch of course, but Spanish or French) to have been imitated in other places. Who is right? Costerius in his own time, perhaps, and Elias for the eighteenth century, when French spread among the upper classes of the Southern Netherlands.

VIII

The movements for standardization and purity are likely to have made people in the Netherlands, as elsewhere in Europe, more aware of impurities and deviations from the norm. At any rate, we find increasing interest in these deviations in the seventeenth and eighteenth centuries. Scholars studied not only dialect but also slang, jargon or what some linguists call 'sectorial' languages, whether they are understood as expressions of particular subcultures or as a means to their construction.[77]

For example, the jargon of beggars and thieves attracted the attention of many early modern writers. In this respect the *Fielten Vocabulaer* (1563) may be inserted in a series of Italian, English, Spanish and French texts such as the *Nuovo modo de intendere la lingua zerga* (1545), the *Caveat for Common Cursitors* (1566) *Romances de Germanía* (1609) and *Jargon de l'argot réformé* (1628). Sailors are another nomadic group that developed a distinctive language, studied in Wigardus van Winschooten's *Seeman* (1681), as well as by later scholars.[78]

Again, it was (and is) possible to identify not only the inhabitants of particular cities but even particular quarters by their language. As in the case of the Cockneys of Bow, the speech of the 'Haarlemmerdykers' of Amsterdam, for instance, betrayed their origins.[79] Some modern studies suggest that religious groups, from English Puritans and Quakers to German Pietists, could be recognized by their distinctive sociolects, ranging from vocabulary to accent.[80] It has even been suggested that Protestants were responsible for the 'delight in the diminutive' perceptible to this day in the Netherlands (as in Scotland, another Calvinist culture).[81]

The language of peasants also engaged the attention of urban scholars in this period. Lambert ten Kate noted in 1723 (as Vincenzo Borghini and Georg Stiernhjelm had already pointed out in the cases of Italian and Swedish) that peasants spoke Dutch in a more archaic manner than townspeople ('vind men de Spraek bij den Boer altijd ouderwetscher dan bij de Steêman').[82]

What we sometimes call 'bureaucratese' or the 'jargon' of lawyers was already attracting unsympathetic interest in the Dutch Republic as it was doing elsewhere in early modern Europe. Thus Thomas Asselijn wrote of *Stadthuiswoorden*, while the *Onderzoeker* referred to *advocaten-Duitsch* in 1771. The jargon was criticized in part because it was unintelligible to the laity, in part because it included many foreign words. Thus Nicolaus Stenius condemned 'Advocaets ende Procureurs Duytsch' as 'een mengelmoes uyt verscheide talen, maer uyt de Latijnsche principael'[83]

As I suggested earlier, the language of gender, especially the language of women, seems to have been neglected in the case of Dutch, compared with recent work on early modern English, French and Italian. A systematic examination of comedies from this point of view might yield valuable information. Other kinds of text also contain scraps of information of the same kind, for instance Richard Dafforne's reference to 'onze juffrouwenspraak' in his guide to spelling of 1627, or Simon van Leeuwen's description in his *Batavia Illustrata* (1685) of 'de lispende en kromtongde wyven, de regte grondtaal verbabbelen'.[84] A more intense use of letters and trial records might flesh out the picture. The importance of French as the language of instruction in boarding schools for young ladies in Bruges, Ypres and elsewhere in the later eighteenth century is known, but the extent to which upper-class women as well as men in the Netherlands, North and South, spoke French in the seventeenth and eighteenth centuries, and in what circumstances, requires further investigation.[85]

Finally, and most controversially, there is the question of the language of class. Is the concern with 'U and non-U' a uniquely English one? Surely not, even if the English are unusually preoccupied, not to say obsessed, with the topic.[86] Van der Wal notes, for instance, that Vondel's famous remarks about The Hague and Amsterdam as linguistic models explicitly refer only to 'lieden van goede opvoedinghe'.[87] Again, Daan has drawn attention to Lambert ten Kate's remarks on the use of the third person in polite society 'Heeft mijn Heer dat verrigt?' (a device still employed in Poland and Portugal today), and also on the way in which *Je* and *We* were replacing *Gy* and *Wy*. He has also noted Justus van Effen's distinctions in speech between different classes, generations and situations as well as between different regions.[88] Van der Sijs has noted that the pronunciation of *hand* as *hongd* 'wordt ... in de hele zeventiende eeuw gebruikt als stereotiep voor de Hollandse laagste klasse'.[89]

Eighteenth-century condemnations of *straattaal* or *straat-Duitsch* also suggest that a conscious link was made between language and social class[90] The poet Ludocus Smids uses the term and explains it in 1694 in his *Het Toetsteentje der Nederduytsche Toneel*. In 1708, Séwel wrote of 'den gemeenen spreektrant ... dat men straattaal vermyde'. Ten Kate took up the term in 1723.[91] He also noted that 'in groote Steden, vind man eenig onderscheid in dat stuk tusschen Hooge, Middelbare, en Lage Gemeente'.[92] As a writer from Utrecht remarked, there was a great difference 'tusschen de uitspraek van voornaeme en beschaefde lieden, gemeente burgers en het grauw'.[93]

IX

As the footnotes to this essay make clear, a considerable body of work on the social history of Dutch is already in existence. The value of different kinds of sources has been assessed, and work is under way on the relatively neglected domains of private letters by ordinary people and the testimonies of witnesses in courts.

The most important shift of interpretation in the last generation, in tune with developments in other domains of historical writing, is a shift from a single to a multiple perspective. What used to be seen as the relatively simple, unilinear story of the rise of standard Dutch (thanks in particular to the translation of the Bible into the vernacular), is now presented as considerably more complicated and contested. A single 'grand narrative' of the triumph of the vernacular has been replaced by a more pluralist approach linked to the increasing interest in cultural hybridity. In the case of language, this means paying more attention than before to the survival of dialects and sociolects. It also means focusing more sharply on the acceptance by many speakers of words taken from foreign languages – Latin, French, German, English, and even Arabic and Malay – as well as to the reaction by purists against the consequent 'contamination' of Dutch.

There remains a gap between historians, many of whom do not yet take language seriously, and linguists, some of whom concentrate on developments internal to language. As we have seen, the Dutch historians who have written about changes in language are relatively few. Again, only a few Dutch linguists have so far made use of the work of social historians, or of historical sociologists such as Norbert Elias. This lack of communication between disciplines is not peculiar to the Netherlands. On the contrary, it has many parallels in other countries and remains a major obstacle to the understanding of cultural change. To attempt to close or at least to reduce this gap between disciplines, so far as one particular cluster of problems is concerned, has been one of the principal aims of this exploratory essay.

Notes

* This text is the revised version of a lecture given at the Meertens Instituut on March 10, 2005. My thanks to the audience for their questions and comments. For encouragement, advice, comments on the draft, references and books I should also like to thank, *inter alia*, Marcel Bax, Karel Bostoen, Willem Frijhoff, Joop Goudsblom, Peter Jan Margry, Marc van Oostendorp, Pieter van Reenen, Herman Roodenburg, Rachel Selbach and Marijke van der Wal.
1. Peter Burke and Roy Porter (eds.), *The Social History of Language* (Cambridge, 1987).
2. Nicoline van der Sijs, *Taal als mensenwerk: het onstaan van het ABN* (Amsterdam, 2004), 102-3.
3. John B. Pride, *New Englishes* (Rowley, Mass., 1982); Gunnel Melcher and Philip Shaw, *World Englishes* (London, 2003).
4. On developments in the South I am particularly indebted to Roland Willemyns, *Het verhaal van het Vlaams: De geschiedenis van het Nederlands in de Zuidelijke Nederlanden* (Antwerp and Utrecht, 2003).
5. Cf. Peter Burke, *Languages and Communities in Early Modern Europe* (Cambridge, 2004).
6. David Leith, *A Social History of English* (1983, second ed. London 1997); Richard W. Bailey, *Images of English: A Cultural History of the Language* (Ann Arbor, 1991).
7. Leopold Peeters, *Taalopbouw als Renaissance Ideal* (Amsterdam, 1990), 92.
8. Lesley Milroy, *Language and Social Networks* (Oxford, 1980).
9. On the invisible hand, see Rudi Keller, *Sprachwandel. Von der unsichtbaren Hand in der Sprache* (Tübingen, 1990). Agency is stressed in Milroy, *Language*.
10. Jo Daan, 'Sociolecten in de 18de eeuw', in José Cajot, Ludger Kremer and Hermann Niebaum (eds.) *Lingua Theodisca* (Münster, 1995), 263-9.
11. Andries A. Verdenius, *Bredero's Dialectkunst als Hollandse Reaktie tegen zuidnederlandse taalhegemonie* (Groningen, 1933); Jo Daan, 'Sociolecten en stijlen bij Bredero', *Spektator* 14, no. 4 (1985), 254-60, at 254.
12. For example, the texts preserved in the British Public Record Office and soon to be studied in detail by Dutch scholars. On one sailor, Leendert Koelmans, *Het Nederlands van Michiel de Ruyter: morfologie, woordvorming, syntaxis* (Assen, 2001).

13. Peeters, *Taalopbouw*, 111; examples in Marijke van der Wal and Cor van Bree, *Geschiedenis van het Nederlands* (Utrecht, 1992), 223-5.
14. Marcel Bax and Nanne Streekstra, 'Civil Rites: Ritual Politeness in Early Modern Dutch Letter-Writing', *Journal of Historical Pragmatics* 4 (2003), 303-26.
15. Pieter van Reenen and Maaike Mulder, 'Linguistic Interpretation of Spelling Variation', in Michèle Goyens and Werner Verbeke (eds.) *The Dawn of the Written Vernacular in Western Europe* (Leuven, 2003), 179-99.
16. Franciscus P.H. Prick van Wely, *Der Verindisching van ons Nederlandsch* (Batavia and The Hague, 1903); Joop van den Berg, *Soebatten, Sarongs en Sinjo's: Indische woorden in het Nederlands* (The Hague, 1990).
17. C.G.N. de Vooys, *Geschiedenis van de Nederlandse taal* (1931: 5th edn, Antwerp-Groningen 1952). Cf. L. van den Branden, *Het streven naar verheerlijking, zuivering en opbouw van het Nederlands in de 16de eeuw* (Ghent, 1956).
18. On language contact in the Southern Netherlands, Willemyns, *Vlaams*, 161-2.
19. Daan, 'Bredero'; id., 'Sociolecten in de 18de eeuw'; Peeters, *Taalopbouw*; Willem Frijhoff, 'Verfransing? Franse taal en Nederlandse cultuur tot in de revolutietijd', *Bijdragen en Mededelingen tot de Geschiedenis van der Nederlanden* 104 (1989), 592-609.
20. Van der Wal and van Bree, *Nederlands*; Willemyns, *Vlaams*; Marijke van der Wal, *De moedertaal centraal: standardisatie-aspecten in de Nederlanden omstreeks 1650* (The Hague, 1995); Van der Sijs, *Taal*.
21. Among them W. Vandenbussche, author of *Een bijdrage tot de studie van het taalgebruik van de lagere klassen in het 19de-eeuwse Brugge* (Brussel, 1999)
22. Van den Branden, *Verheerlijking*; A.M. Hagen (ed.) *O schone moedertaal: lofzangen op het Nederlands, 1500-2000* (Amsterdam, 1999). Stevin's *Uytspraeck vande weerdigheyt der Duytsche tael* was published as introductory chapter to his book *De beghinselen der weeghconst*.
23. Burke, *Languages*, 68-9.
24. Van der Wal, *Moedertaal*, 36ff, discusses this phenomenon in terms of 'functieuitbreding'.
25. Charles A.J. Armstrong, 'The Language Question in the Low Countries', in John R. Hale, Roger Highfield and Beryl Smalley (eds.), *Europe in the Late Middle Ages* (London, 1965), pp.386-409: cf. Willemyns, *Vlaams*, 95-106.

26. Cor van Bree, 'The Development of So-called Town Frisian', in Peter Bakker and Maarten Mous (eds.) *Mixed Languages* (Amsterdam, 1994), 69-82.
27. J.W. Muller, 'De uitbreiding van ons taalgebied in de zeventiende eeuw', *Nieuwe Taalgids* 15 (1921), 161-93, 245-60, 298-309.
28. Peter Trudgill, 'Third-Person Singular Zero', 1997: rpr Jacek Fisiak and Peter Trudgill (eds.) *East Anglian English* (Cambridge, 2001), pp. 179-86.
29. R. van der Meulen, *De Hollandsche Zee- en Scheepstermen in het Russisch* (Amsterdam, 1909); id, *Nederlandsche Woorden in het Russisch* (Amsterdam, 1959).
30. Maurice Aymard (ed.) *Dutch Capitalism and World Capitalism* (Cambridge, 1982).
31. Franciscus P.H. Prick van Wely, *Neerlands Taal in 't verre Osten* (Semarang, 1906); Kees Groeneboer, *Gateway to the West: the Dutch Language in Colonial Indonesia, 1600-1950* (Amsterdam, 1998).
32. Frits Vos, 'De Nederlandse taal in Japan', in Leo G. Dalhuisen and H. J. M. van der Geest (eds.) *Deshima, een factorij en Japan* (Bloemendaal, 1985), 34; Donald Keene, *The Japanese Discovery of Europe 1720-1830* (1952), revised edn Stanford 1969; Grant K. Goodman, *Japan: the Dutch Experience* (1967), revised edn *Japan and the Dutch, 1600-1853* (Richmond, VA, 2000).
33. Groeneboer, *Gateway*; Edith Raidt, 'Nederlandse en Afrikaanse spreektaal in die 17de en 18de eeu', rpr her *Historiese Taalkunde: Studies oor die geskiedenis van Afrikaans* (Johannesburg, 1994), 53-71; id., *Einführung in Geschichte und Struktur des Afrikaans* (Darmstadt, 1983).
34. On the North, Frijhoff, 'Verfransing?'; on the South, Marcel Deneckere, *Histoire de la langue française dans les Flandres* (Ghent, 1954). On other parts of Europe, Burke, *Languages*.
35. Peter Burke, 'Translation into Latin in Early Modern Europe', in Peter Burke and Ronnie Hsia (eds.) *Cultures of Translation in Early Modern Europe* (forthcoming, Cambridge 2006).
36. Wal and Bree, *Nederlands*, 188.
37. On different concepts of standardization, Wal, *Moedertaal*, 1.
38. 'Smeltkroes': Van der Sijs, *Taal*, 31.
39. Willemyns, *Vlaams*, 106; Van der Sijs, *Taal*.
40. According to a forthcoming paper by Hans Bennis, the reflexive system came into Dutch from the eastern dialects.
41. Van der Wal, *Moedertaal*, 32.

42. Elizabeth Eisenstein, *The Printing Press as an Agent of Change* (Cambridge, 1979); for criticisms, Adrian Johns, 'How to Acknowledge a Revolution', in *American Historical Review* 107 (2002), 106-25; for a balanced survey, David McKitterick, *Print, Manuscript and the Search for Order, 1450-1830* (Cambridge, 2003).
43. Burke, *Languages*, 106-7.
44. A.A. Weijnen, *Het Algemeen Beschaafd Nederlands Historisch Beschouwd* (Assen, 1974), 3; Willemyns, *Vlaams*, 109-11.
45. Weijnen, *ABN*; Willemyns, *Vlaams*, 111.
46. Quoted in Leopold Peeters, *Taalopbouw*, 76.
47. Burke, *Languages*.
48. Quoted in De Vooys, *Nederlandse taal*, 60. Cf. Aurelius A. Den Hollander, *De Nederlandse bijbelvertalingen 1522-1545* (Nieuwkoop, 1997).
49. Andrew Pettegree, *Emden and the Dutch Revolt* (Oxford, 1992), 90.
50. Doede Nauta, *De Statenvertaling 1637-1937* (Haarlem, 1937); A.C. de Gooyer, *Bijbeltaal en moedertaal: de invloed van de Statenvertaling op het Nederlands* (The Hague, 1962); J. van Delden, *De Tale Kanaäns: Bijbelse woorden, spreekwoorden en uitdrukkingen* (Nijkerk, 1982). A dissenting note is expressed in Robert B. Howell (2000) 'The Low Countries', in Stephen Barbour and Cathy Carmichael (eds.), *Language and Nationalism in Europe* (Oxford, 2000), 130-50. A recent overview in Van der Sijs, *Taal*, 113-52
51. De Vooys, *Nederlandse taal*, 139
52. Matthijs Siegenbeek, *Verhandeling over de Nederduitsche spelling* (Amsterdam, 1804); cf. Van der Sijs, *Taal*, 215-94; cf. Willemyns, *Vlaams*, 123-4.
53. De Vooys, *Nederlandse taal*, 87; Wal and Bree, *Nederlands*, 220.
54. Quoted Willemyns, *Vlaams*, 140.
55. De Vooys, *Nederlandse taal*, 117.
56. Bakker and Mous, *Mixed Languages*; Burke, *Languages*, 111-40.
57. Herman Roodenburg, *The Eloquence of the Body: Perspectives on Gesture in the Dutch Republic* (Zwolle, 2005), 47.
58. Lois M. Feister (1973) 'Linguistic Communication between the Dutch and the Indians in New Netherland, 1609-64', *Ethnohistory* 20 (1973), 25-38.
59. In the case of English, for instance, it is possible to turn to Richard Wermser, *Statistische Studien zur Entwicklung des englischen Wortschatzes* (Berlin, 1976), and to Terttu Nevaainen, 'Lexis and Semantics', in Roger Lass (ed.) *History of the English Language*, vol. 3 (Cambridge, 1999),

332-458. For Dutch, see Nicoline de Van der Sijs, 'Etymologie in het digitale tijdperk' (Ph.D. thesis, University of Leiden, 2001).
60. Prick van Wely, *Verindisching*; Van den Berg, *Soebatten*.
61. Nicoline van der Sijs (ed.) *Taaltrots: purisme in een veertigtal talen* (Amsterdam, 1999).
62. Van der Sijs, *Taal*, especially 108ff, 356ff, 368ff.
63. Mary Douglas, *Purity and Danger* (London, 1966).
64. Simon Schama, *The Embarrassment of Riches* (London, 1987), 375-93.
65. Burke, *Languages*, 150-1.
66. Van den Branden, *Verheerlijking*, 205; Van der Sijs, *Taal*, 370-3.
67. Hagen, *Moedertaal*, 278; Van der Wal, *Moedertaal*, 56, 72, 95; Van der Sijs, *Taal*, 67, 328, 37.
68. Willemyns, *Vlaams*, 121; Van der Sijs, *Taal*, 99.
69. De Vooys, *Nederlandse taal*, 132; cf. Burke, *Languages*, 120-1.
70. On Stevin, Van den Branden, *Verheerlijking*, 188-209; Van der Sijs, *Taal*, 311-18.
71. Guido Bentivoglio, *Historie der Nederlantsche oorlogen* (Amsterdam, 1674).
72. M. Jelínek, 'Český jazykový purismus v dějinách kultury novodobé spisovné češtiny', in *Jakykové actuality* 22 (1985), 113-17. When I made this distinction in Burke, *Languages*, I was unaware of Jelínek's article. The history of scholarship is unfortunately full of such re-inventions.
73. Norbert Elias, *The Civilizing Process* (1939, English trans., 2 vols., Oxford 1981-2), 'excursus on the modelling of speech at court'; cf. Peter Burke, 'Language in the Civilizing Process', forthcoming in *Figurations* (2005).
74. Joop Goudsblom, 'Het Algemeen Beschaafd Nederlands' (1964), rpr *Taal en sociale werkelijkheid*, Amsterdam 1988, 11-29; cf. W.G. Hellinga (1938) *De opbouw van de algemeen-beschaafde uitspraak van het Nederlands*, rpr in *Bijdragen tot de geschiedenis van de Nederlandse taalcultuur* (Arnhem, 1968); Howell, 'Low Countries'.
75. Bax and Streekstra, 'Civil rites'.
76. Peter Burke, *The Art of Conversation* (Cambridge, 1993); id., *The Fortunes of the Courtier* (Cambridge, 1995); Anna Bryson, *From Courtesy to Civility: Changing Codes of Conduct in Early Modern England* (Oxford, 1998), especially 151-92; Benedetta Craveri, *La civiltà della conversazione* (Milan, 2001); Roodenburg, *Eloquence*.
77. Gian Luigi Beccaria, *I linguaggi settoriali in Italia* (Milan, 1973); Peter Burke and Roy Porter (eds.) *Languages and Jargons* (Cambridge, 1995), especially the introduction; Burke, *Languages*, 15-42.

78. E.g. J.H. Roeding, *Allgemeines Wörterbuch der Marine* (4 vols., Hamburg 1794-8). On Winschooten, Van der Sijs, *Taal*, 363-4. Cf. Leendert Koelmans, *Zeemans Lexicon: word en woordbetekenis bij Michiel de Ruyter* (Zutphen, 1997).
79. Herman Roodenburg, 'Naar een etnografie van de vroegmoderne stad: De "gebuyrten" in Leiden en Den Haag', in Peter te Boekhorst, Peter Burke and Willem Frijhoff (eds.) *Cultuur en maatschappij in Nederland 1500-1850. Een historisch-antropologisch perspectief* (Meppel and Amsterdam, 1992), 219-243, at 231.
80. August Langer, *Der Wortschatz des Deutschen Pietismus* (Tübingen 1954); Marinus van Beek, *An Enquiry into Puritan Vocabulary* (Groningen, 1969); Richard Bauman, *Let Your Words be Few: Symbolism of Speech and Silence among the Quakers* (Cambridge, 1983).
81. J.M. Bulloch, 'The Delight of the Doric in the Diminutive', in William A. Craigie (ed.) *The Scottish Tongue* (London 1924), 127-51.
82. Ten Kate quoted in Leopold Peeters, *Taalopbouw*, 14; comparisons in Burke, *Languages*, 23.
83. De Vooys, *Nederlandse taal*, 112, 117, 138.
84. Quoted in Van der Sijs, *Taal*, 160 and Peeters, *Taalopbouw*, 166-7.
85. Deneckere, *Langue française*, 35-6.
86. Alan Ross, 'Linguistic Class-Indicators in Present-Day English', *Neuphilologische Mitteilungen* 55 (1954) 20-56; Nancy Mitford (ed.) *Noblesse Oblige* (London, 1956).
87. Van der Wal, *Moedertaal*, 33.
88. Daan, 'Sociolecten in de 18de eeuw', 263-5.
89. Van der Sijs, *Taal*, 159.
90. Langendijk (1721) and the *Onderzoeker* (1771), quoted in De Vooys, *Nederlandse taal*, 129, 138; Séwel quoted in Van der Sijs, *Taal*, 366.
91. A.M. Hagen, 'Taal- en stilniveaus in achtiende-eeuws Nederlands', in Cajot, Kremer and Niebaum, *Lingua Theodisca*, 271-81, at 275-6.
92. Quoted in Peeters, *Taalopbouw*, 14.
93. Quoted in Hellinga, *Opbouw*, 327-8.